31 Days
with
Me and God

THE JOURNEY OF MY HEART

Keisha L. Wells

Author: Keisha L. Wells
Publication Services–Kingdom News Publication
Services, LLC.

DISCLAIMER
All the material contained in this book is provided for
educational and informational purposes only. No
responsibility can be taken for any results or outcomes
resulting from the use of this material.
While every attempt has been made to provide
information that is both accurate and effective, the
author does not assume any responsibility for the
accuracy or use/misuse of this information.

Printed in the United States of America.
ISBN 978-0-998026282

KINGDOM NEWS TODAY
Publication Services, LLC

Table of Contents

Day 1: It's you...No, it's me. 1

Day 2: Forgiveness if for you NOT them!.............. 5

Day 3: Heart Motives, Are they pure?.................. 7

Day 4: Focus 9

Day 5: A Thankful Heart.....................................13

Day 6: To Whom am I Committed? 16

Day 7: Perseverance.. 18

Day 8: Dear 2016...20

Day 9: Eight means New Beginnings 21

Day 10: New Beginnings Part Two..................... 22

Day 11: With Loving-Kindness have I Drawn You 25

Day 12: Embracing My Journey.......................... 27

Day 13: Why I Kissed Online Dating Goodbye.... 29

Day 14: As I Continue to Wait............................. 33

Day 15: I Need Jesus... 35

Day 16: 30 Years and Counting........................... 37

Day 17: Sorry, Not Sorry 39

Day 18: Happy 1 Year #WifeinTraining.............. 41

Day 19: Letter to My Husband 43

Day 20: Tunnel Vision 45

Day 21: Reflection Revealed Many Victories.......47

Day 22: Hello LOVE..49

Day 23: Love is more than a feeling 52

Day 24: #theUnmasking 54

Day 25: Saying I Love You 56

Day 26: A Prideful Heart....................................59

Day 27: Marriage 60

Day 28: It's Been A While...Hey Y'all! 62

Day 29: This Can't Be Real..................................65

Day 30: Remain Silent, He will Fight for You 68

Day 31: It's Been Over A Week........................... 71

About the Author 73

Day 1

It's you... No, it's me.

October 11, 2016

Being honest with oneself can be a difficult process to go through. Looking at oneself in the mirror and seeing the ugly truth about one's character can bring up emotions that are uncomfortable. I'm learning that it is in those most uncomfortable moments are the ones that bring the most healing. The process of getting to know someone is not just about getting to know that person; it is also about getting to know what things are deeply rooted within your soul in order to heal from the inside out. If it was not for my relationship with the Holy Spirit, I would be taking my internal uncomfortableness out on the individuals who are close to my heart.

This season of my life has been the most uncomfortable season I've been through since I started my walk with Jesus Christ. I'm learning to be content with being uncomfortable. Like the Apostle Paul said, "Not that I speak from want, for I have learned to be content in whatever circumstance I am." Philippians 4:11 NSAB. Why am I content with being uncomfortable? Because the more uncomfortable I am is a

1

sign that I am in the will of God. Even with the uncomfortableness, I still have a "Yes Lord" within my spirit.

Let's talk about being uncomfortable! I was talking to this guy who I really was digging. He was tall (6'3"), dark chocolate skin tone, and just handsome! His physique was everything I desired in a man. I liked everything about him: he was smart, creative, optimistic, and a go-getter. There was only one thing that turned me off about him: he ghosted me- not once, not twice, but THREE times! He really hurt my feelings. I forgave him and moved on. Honestly, I should have just forgiven him then moved on with my life. I didn't and the situation I placed myself in with him left me completely uncomfortable. When a man shows me, he was not interested in me anymore, I move on with my life and won't think of him anymore; however, I know there was some things within me that needed to be purged and I needed to be humbled.

I know you're probably thinking, "Cousin, why did you accept him back?!?" Well, I know I did not have to accept him back into my life. I did because I believed he was my husband, the man God had for me. You can say I took a risk believing God... that he was the one for me. So, I allowed him back into my life. Now, I know that God's will is not for me to be involved with a person who is toxic/ unhealthy for me.

I'm learning that taking risks during this uncomfortable season is the only way I am going to continue to grow in every area of my life. Marriage will soon be my reality. Being uncomfortable while being prepared for my husband and our family is well worth it. This is only just the foundational work being done through prayer, fasting, and being content with being uncomfortable. Every other season that I've gone through that was uncomfortable was worth it. I know that God will never have me enter a season without an expected end.

October is a month of heavenly release, heavenly outpouring, overpowering the enemy, opulence (in every area of my life), wealth, abundance, and lavish supply. I am a Saint on Steroids (SOS).

I am expecting God to move in a supernatural way in my life-not just for the month of October, but for the rest of my life. Wealth and riches are in my house. Prosperity is in my house. I am declaring and decreeing that I will have a happy, holy, healthy, and prosperous marriage in the name of Jesus Christ. Amen!

Shalom & Agape,

Keisha

Answer these questions:

Have you ever been in a place where you were extremely uncomfortable, but it was a place you needed to be in order to heal from certain things?

How did you feel going through the process?

Are you glad that you are able to look back on the process and see the growth?

Day 2

Forgiveness is for you, NOT them!

October 23, 2016

Over the last 10 years, I've learned that forgiveness is not for the person who have wronged me. Forgiveness is for me. Throughout my life, I have been in many situations where offense has taken me through some severe emotional rollercoasters. I had to learn how to forgive others daily for the things they have done towards me. Sometimes the individual that had offended me did not even know they caused any type of offense. Another reason why unforgiveness was toxic to me is because it allowed room for the adversary. Unforgiveness in my heart allowed bitterness, anger, frustration, strife, envy, jealousy, and everything else in-between to distort my thinking and perception which causes dysfunction. If I'm telling the Holy Spirit He is welcome to come reside in me and I'm dealing with things like bitterness, anger, strife, envy, and jealousy, I believe it makes Him uncomfortable. The beautiful thing about the love of God is that He will not allow you to remain in that place if you desire freedom in that area. For me, I wanted that freedom. That is when the Holy Spirit began to work on me with the unforgiveness that was trying to run rampant within my soul, spirit, and heart. I had to break free from those things that were trying to hinder me.

I had to accept that I do not have control over people's actions. I only control how I chose to respond to those individuals. I had to forgive them just like my Father in Heaven has forgiven me of many things. I also had to forgive myself. Jesus the Christ had a forgiving heart. Why can't I have the same heart? If I'm made in the image of God, I should display the same type of forgiveness and love He has extended towards me... RIGHT?!?

Now, I'm in a place where forgiveness with the help of Holy Spirit comes to me in greater measure. My heart has remained open with His help. Forgiving others will put your heart in a posture to receive more of God's love. Recently, I have experienced just that. I had to forgive even if the individual did not apologize. Forgiveness is for me, not the other person. Now that my heart is in a posture to receive more of the love of God for myself, I can reciprocate the same type of love God has given and shown me.

I will close with this verse: "And be kind to one another, tender-hearted forgiving each other, just as God in Christ also had forgiven you." Ephesians 4:32 NASB

Shalom & Agape,

Keisha

Day 3

Heart Motives, Are they pure?

November 9, 2016

I'm learning that not every heart desire is pure. There have been times when my heart motives were all wrong after the Holy Spirit identified it. I'm learning that it is so important to continue to do regular heart checks by asking the Holy Spirit to reveal what is in my heart. I can remember a time when I hated doing heart checks because I was not ready to see what was going to be revealed to me. I would never pray, "Search my heart, oh God." Reflecting on that revealed that I had a prideful heart and I was walking in fear. First off, God HATES a prideful heart. Secondly, God has not given me the spirit of fear. Both are of the flesh/carnality. Yet, I was still saying I love God with all my heart. Sounds crazy, huh? It was crazy. Wicked and deceitful heart? That I had. Jeremiah 17:9-10 NASB states, "The heart is more deceitful than all else and is desperately sick (wicked); Who can understand it?" Then the next verse brings it home, "I, the LORD, search the heart,

I test the mind, even to give to each man according to his ways, according to the results of his deeds."

So, you mean to tell me that the LORD God searches my heart, tests my mind, and then gives to me according to my ways. Help me, Holy Ghost. Sowing and reaping. I told Him, "King Jesus, when you're sitting enthroned on my heart, I desire for it to be a comfy place for you." I seriously mean that. Allowing the Holy Spirit to reveal the ugly truth about my heart motives, the impurities, wickedness and how deceitful my heart can be, has brought many tears. The question that remained was how and when did this take place? The answer: I was born into sin. I had to be born again of the Spirit and water baptism. Now, I can confidently go to the throne of my Lord Savior and ask for forgiveness then repent-turn away and move forward.

Now, my prayer is this, "Create in me a clean heart, O God, and renew a steadfast spirit within me." Psalms 51:10 NASB My heart's desire is it remains pure before God by doing regular heart checks that include praying, fasting, and reading my Bible. These four things have helped me face some very ugly truths regarding my heart motives.

I am committing to daily heart checks, praying, fasting (from something), and reading the Bible to ensure that I am in a place to hear God speak to me concerning my heart motives. I pray that this has encouraged you in some way.

Shalom & Agape,

Keisha

Day 4

FOCUS

November 19, 2016

"You have been distracted; get back focused." Reading those words from a text message I received the first day of Yesvember (11-1-2016) made me cry internally. I looked to others for answers. They were just as puzzled as I was. Now that I'm looking back at this, I should have looked to the Holy Spirit for answers that would have saved me from trying to process things on my own. From that, I am continuing to learn that God seriously searches the heart. Man, only sees what God allows them to discern (see).

I went through four different stages of facing TRUTH in a week. Someone years ago, said something to me so profound: "I may look like I have it all together, but I've got issues." Yeah, that was me at the beginning of Yesvember. The first stage of facing TRUTH for me was denial. I denied, denied, denied until I finally accepted the truth of those words from

God (who knows all things about me). Then, I became so angry at myself for allowing distraction to come my way. I guess anger can be considered the second stage of facing TRUTH. I didn't know I was distracted. I was going to church, being actively involved in ministry, being the "good" Christian woman, etc. (That is all works. God cares more about the condition of my heart than works during this season). Oh, how my heart had deceived me. To top it off, I told myself, "Well, they don't know what they are talking about. I don't have to receive every prophetic word spoken to me." The nerve of me to say something so STUPID. That sounds like pride to me. Thank God for conviction! I repented. Thank God for wrapping Himself in a body, sending His Son Jesus Christ (Yeshua Ha-Mashiach), and Holy Spirit.

I consider the third stage of facing TRUTH acceptance. I had to accept the ugly truth of my deceitful heart. Once I finally accepted the TRUTH of my heart condition, I was able to understand even more why King David in Psalm 51:10 NASB wrote, "Create in me a clean heart, O God; and renew a right spirit within me." It's something about being able to accept the condition of my heart. It is very humbling. God loves me so much that He will not allow me to remain in that place of being deceived and unfocused. The love of the Father is so refreshing. It brings much peace to my soul and spirit. Finally, I repented. I turned away after asking God to forgive me for not remaining focused on the correct things. 2 Corinthians 7:10a NASB say, "For the sorrow that is according to the will of God produces a repentance without regret, leading to salvation." I have to continue to work out my own salvation with fear and trembling according to Philippians 2:12c NASB. The fourth and final stage of facing TRUTH is repentance. The word that was released to me on 11-1-2016 did just that.

Before ending this entry, I have decided to do something a little different. I am going to add the questions I asked the Holy Spirit for the last two weeks. After quieting my soul and spirit, I was able to hear His voice clear.

So, here goes...
Me: How could this happen?
Holy Spirit: You allowed your focus to be on the situation.
Me: Who/What got me distracted?
Holy Spirit: You. Your heart was focusing on the wrong things that caused you to be distracted.

Thank you, Heavenly Father, for searching my heart, getting me back on track, and continuing to love on me. Thank you for making things plain. Thank you for clarity. Thank you for understanding. Thank you for wisdom. Thank you for sending Your Son Jesus in order for me to have a relationship with You. Thank you, good, good Father!

My heart's desire is to remain focused and pure before God. I pray that this blesses you in some capacity.

Shalom & Agape,

Keisha

SIDE NOTE:
Yesvember was a prophetic word released over Glorious Triumphant Church, the ministry that I am a part of. For the month of November every previous NO will be YES. Hence, Yesvember. Yesvember came from Pierre the Poet. November= Yesvember.

Day 5

A Thankful Heart

November 26, 2016

I have so much to be thankful for this year: both of my parents are alive and healthy and I have a job that provides a financial resource; however, I am truly thankful for the Holy Spirit. He has been the one who has comforted me on many nights. He has been the one who guided me through many tough times within the last five years. He has also been the one who has shown me myself, loved on me, and gave me an understanding of why I behave the way I do at times. Honestly, I depend wholeheartedly on the Holy Spirit to guide me daily. With His leading and guidance, my heart has learned to remain thankful in all things. Truth be told, it hasn't always been that way. I never really verbalize much; I was the one who would internalize everything. I kept a lot of things bottled in and I complained to myself. Once, I began being thankful for everything - even the bad. I started seeing the glass half-full instead of half-empty.

In the last month and a half, a few things took place that I did not understand why they unfolded the way they did. Looking back at the situation, I am so thankful things did unfold the way they did because I was able to see the truth. Honestly, I was headed down a road of destruction. You see, I was involved with this young man whom I believed was my husband. Did we talk about marriage? Absolutely. Did we ask each other the tough questions? Yes, we did. However, we still struggled with conversing with one another effectively during the most awkward times of us being together. What led to things changing between us was when I shared a dream, I had of him. Was it bad timing to share? Probably. At that time, I thought it was okay to share the dream with him. Afterwards our relationship turned for the worst. I thought we were going to talk about the dream and have an adult conversation about it. Nope, that did not happen. I was hurt because I thought we were better than that. It was the Holy Spirit who saved me even though I experienced hurt emotions/feelings. This is why I'm so thankful for the Holy Spirit guiding and comforting me.

Here are other things I'm thankful for:
- I am thankful for the people God has placed in my life who have the ability to pour into me as I pour into others.
- I am thankful for even unanswered prayers. Why? Because I prayed prayers years ago that if God answered, I would be miserable.
- I am thankful for the ministry that I am a part of. I am thankful for the sound biblical teaching that I get. I am thankful that my Pastor is spirit lead.

14

- I am very thankful for the Holy Spirit pushing me beyond some places I did not want to be pushed into.

It brings me great joy to know that the Greater One lives within me. My heart is thankful for the Holy Spirit, because He is always working with me, through me, and for me.
Tell me, what are some things you are grateful/thankful for?

Shalom & Agape,

Keisha

Day 6

To Whom am I Committed?

December 3, 2016

As the Holy Spirit is continuing to prepare me for the lifelong commitment to my husband, I have to be committed to Jesus Christ the Bridegroom before anyone else. How committed am I to the Bridegroom? Is my heart fully committed to Him? Am I committed to Him only when I feel like it? If I'm not fully committed to the Bridegroom Jesus Christ, how can I commit to my husband? I can't. Not only that, why would I want to commit myself to a man who is not fully committed to Jesus Christ? Nah, I'm good. I will not be doing that. That is a recipe for destruction. I will be getting married only once in this lifetime. That is why Jesus Christ has to be the head of his life and mine. We both have to be fully committed to Him in order to be fully committed to one another. Jesus at the center of it all!

Over the past five years, there have been many times where I wanted to just throw in the towel and not remain committed to Him, but there was someone always praying for me. I could feel the prayers of God's people. There was always an unexplainable drawing that would hit that I could not shake. I would tell myself, "Why not stay committed to Him? You have nothing to lose." Truth be told, I did not have anything to lose but my life in Him. I seriously have to commit myself daily to Him in everything I do. It may sound weird, but I consult with the Holy Spirit from what to wear for the day to which way to drive to get to a certain place. Just from following the Holy Spirit's directions/instructions, I randomly ran into one of my aunts He told me I was going to see.

My commitment to Jesus Christ is important to me. Why? Because I'm married to Christ. I am in covenant with Jesus Christ. I am in Him and He is in me. I am glued to Him.

Ask yourself, to whom are you committed?

Shalom & Agape,

Keisha

Day 7

Perseverance

December 24, 2016

Perseverance is defined as the continued effort to do or achieve something despite difficulties, failure, or opposition; the action or condition or an instance of persevering; steadfastness.

There's two minutes left in the game. The score is tied. This can be anyone's game. Everyone is tired from both teams, but no one is giving up. The final seconds are here: 5... 4... 3... 2... 1! The final buzzer goes off. You look up at the score and see that your team has won. If people only knew how you were feeling in those last two minutes.... if they could hear the prep talks you were giving yourself. The encouraging words. Telling yourself, "This too shall pass. It's almost over."

I will admit that this has been my life for the past three weeks. I was feeling pressure in every area of my life. While I know

I am complete, have full restoration and victory, it doesn't mean that I will not feel growing pains. Honestly, I don't know what opened in the spirit, but your girl felt the intensity of it. I was yelling "LORD, PLEASE HELP ME." Thanks be unto God for helping me persevere through it. The Holy Spirit definitely gave me endurance in order to persevere through it all. I did notice the things that did not bother me in the past were trying to get the best of me. I felt like I was in the fight of the century. The great thing about having a relationship with the Holy Spirit is that He began to remind me that the victory has already been won. I'm going to be honest - a lot of what's going on with me is more of me getting in the way than the enemy. I am my own worst enemy. I overthink almost everything. I've now released that; I'm releasing every negative word and thought in the name of Jesus. I AM NEW. No more walking in the old. I will allow the Holy Spirit to think for me. I will continue to consult with Him instead of allowing my mind to run rampant like an overflowing dam.

As I continue to persevere and be consistent with my love walk with Jesus, I believe it will help someone in the end. Even if it does not, it has shown me that I can continue to plow through with Holy Spirit.

Shalom & Agape,

Keisha

19

Day 8

Dear 2016

December 31, 2016

Thank You for being a friend. You have taught me many things in the past twelve months. You taught me perseverance. You matured me. You showed me that in those times when I feel like giving up, I need to plow through it. You showed me how to leap over things. You showed me that I can dominate in anything as long as I keep God first in my life. You showed me what a forgiving heart look like. You also showed me how to remain excellent during the tough seasons. I am so grateful for 2016.

Shalom & Agape,

Keisha

Day 9

Eight means New Beginnings

January 8, 2017

2017 New Beginnings

New. Fresh. Refreshing: those are the words I think of when I hear the phrase "new beginnings." I have so much for which to be thankful already, and the year just started. The new beginning of something new has hit my life. Honestly, I don't even know who I was several months ago. I don't even recognize that person. And what in the world was I doing trying to get "cuffed" during the fall season?! Looking back on it now, I needed to be in my lane focusing on my relationship with God. Thank God for the new beginning. I'm so excited about 2017.... to be continued!

Shalom & Agape,

Keisha

Day 10

New Beginnings Part Two

January 28, 2017

Three weeks into the New Year, I've noticed the "feelings" of being in a new year have been slowly fading away. As this happened, I decided that I was not going to allow those feelings to dictate what steps I need to take in order to keep the excitement of the new year flowing. I started thinking about what new beginnings meant. I began to think about how in the beginning, God created the heavens and the earth (Genesis 1:1). I believe that 2017 is the year of new things being created hence new beginnings. I believe that there is much power in the words that comes out of someone's mouth. For me, 2017 is the year of many things coming to pass. How? Well, I'm going to call or speak those things into being which does not exist (Roman 4:17). In the beginning God spoke things into existence. Being that I am made in the image of God, I believe all I have to do is speak in order to create the things I want to see come into existence. Also, death

22

and life are in the power of the tongue (Proverbs 18:21). In this case, it is my tongue. I am going to create LIFE with my words to the things that need to come to life, then DEATH to those things that need to die in my life and others. I'm creating more new beginnings with my words.

As I continue to create new beginning with my words, I'm learning to be even more mindful of what I say. I've never been a person who was a "motor mouth," but I've always been one to have a STRONG opinion about different things. Most of the time when my opinion was not asked, I would volunteer a lot of "wisdom" at the wrong time. I guess I needed to work on being quick to hear and slow to speak (James 1:19). Heck, I need to continue to allow the Holy Spirit to continue to work on me now with that. Facing these hard truths always brings me to my knees before my Lord Savior Jesus Christ. Thank God for new mercies.

Not only am I creating new beginnings for myself with words, I'm also doing it for others. I am creating new beginnings for my future husband, our future children, our future children's children, and for others around me. As I'm creating these new beginnings with my words, my prayer is that pleasant words are a honeycomb, sweet to their souls and healing to their bones (Proverbs 16:24).

I pray that this blesses you just has much it had blessed me while I was writing.

Shalom & Agape,

Keisha

Something to think about:

What type of new beginnings are you creating with your word?

Are you speaking LIFE or DEATH?

To what are you speaking LIFE?

To what are you speaking DEATH?

Are you being mindful of what you say?

Day 11

With Loving-Kindness Have I Drawn You

February 5, 2017

Jeremiah 31:3 states, "With loving-kindness have I drawn you." These are the words that I think of when I'm drawn to people who are loving and kind to me. It's something about knowing when a person has a good heart; however, it is the things that people allow in their lives that will cause a person to not want to be bothered with them. For me, I'm learning to see past what a person's behavior may be at the time and reminding myself that it is not them acting out; it is a spirit operating through them trying to throw me off track and distract me. I can actually see the God in an individual despite what they display. I am absolutely grateful that God has allowed me to see past what a person tries to cover up.

You are probably wondering, "What does this have to do with becoming a wife?" It has a lot to do with becoming a wife for me. I desire children. There are going to be times when my husband and my children are going to behave in a way that may cause me to react that would be unpleasant; however, I know the Holy Spirit will speak to my heart right in that moment to allow me to see what really is going on. If I am unable to see what is going on with my children and husband, I will react to them in a way that may possibly throw the whole household off. It is my job as a wife and mother to manage my household spiritually even though my husband is the head and sets the spiritual temperature in our home. This is where my words and behavior affect what happens next. I have to continue to speak life to those things that need life, and death to those things that are negative influences that need to die. I have to allow loving-kindness to flow in order for my husband, children, and others to be drawn to Christ whom lives within me.

The scripture that speaks volumes to me is Jeremiah 31:3, "The LORD appeared to him from a far saying, "I have loved you with an everlasting love; therefore, I have drawn you with loving-kindness." NASB.

Over six years ago, it was God's loving-kindness towards me that drew my heart towards His. I can imagine hearing God say, "I have loved you with an everlasting love; I have drawn you with loving-kindness." It is something about being pursued by God. I can honestly say His love has chased me down. He chased me to the point that I am on my knees, humbling myself before Him due to his everlasting love towards me. I cry out to Him, "ABBA, Father, thank you for loving on me!"

Shalom & Agape,

Keisha

Day 12

Embracing My Journey

March 5, 2017

As my heart continues to wait, I hear it singing a new song and it's one of contentment. For so long I wasn't embracing my journey of becoming a wife; I looked at it more like a task.... like something that I would be able to mark the box off with an X. I was told that the X usually marks the spot, but in my case it did not. The X in my case kept the journey arm distance away. I was trying to hold on to the little control I had over my life. Truth be told, I still wasn't fully committed to Christ when this process all started. Let me redact that statement: I was fully committed to Christ. I did not trust the process of the journey. My pride is what held me back. Pride is what kept me stuck. Pride is what made me think I had everything figured out. My heart is definitely on a journey of truly being pruned and humility is the only way that will allow me to continue to embrace my journey.

Let me be completely transparent with you: before this journey started my thoughts towards marriage were a little distorted. I wanted to be married because I wanted the physical benefits of it. I mean, having kids is cool. Having someone to split the bills with, cool. Then one day the Holy Spirit revealed to me that marriage is way deeper than that. Marriage is a ministry. To be honest, life is a ministry. It all depends on what type of perspective you want to take on it. Now that my perspective and understanding of marriage is much clearer as well as healthy, embracing my journey has become much easier.

At the end of the day, it was pride that kept me from embracing my journey. I had to change my mindset and get an understanding of what was really going on with me as I continue to embark on my journey. Embracing my journey has taught me that love serves, love waits, love opens, and love is understanding. My question for you is, are you embracing your journey?

Shalom & Agape,

Keisha

Day 13

Why I Kissed Online Dating Goodbye

April 16, 2017

Do you really want to know why I kissed online dating goodbye!? The truth is that I stopped with the online dating stuff due to the fact of becoming **TIRED** of attracting the same type of man: dysfunctional. Yes, this God-fearing woman attracted dysfunctional men! Even though I had been set-free, delivered, lived a consecrated life, I was still born in dysfunction. Even though I did not live out of that particular spirit, it was something that was deeply rooted within my soul. I believe it was a Friday night... I was at Glorious Triumphant Church when the Apostle Stokes spoke a prophetic message saying that, "Every woman that is tired of attracting dysfunctional men, I uproot and rebuke that spirit of dysfunction in the name of Jesus Christ." I do not know about anyone else, but that night I received that within my spirit. I was set-free from that dysfunctional spirit that kept attracting those men. I then began to speak life until the men I attracted changed. I would say to myself, "I attract men who are healthy and whole within their spirit, lives, emotions, finances, and relationships." It took time for me to see the full manifestation of it; however, I have seen the fruit of it.

Reason #2 why I kissed online dating goodbye: I felt like I was looking to be found for all the wrong reasons. I also still had some issues within myself. I still did not understand what being a wife was. It is a lot deeper than what I grew up learning what it meant to be a wife (definitely not discrediting my mom, who is a great example of a wife by the way). However, the more I began to deepen my relationship with God through Jesus Christ by the Holy Spirit, the more He began to show me what it meant to be a Proverbs 31:10-31 wife, 1 Corinthians 7 wife, Titus 2:3-5, 11 woman/wife, and 1 Timothy 3:11 woman.

I guess you can consider reason #3 of why I kissed online dating goodbye was due to the fact that I was showing God in my actions that I wanted to take things into my own hands because I did not trust Him. While I thought God forgot about me, He was taking His sweet time putting the puzzle pieces in place, and your girl was HOT for some attention. It also showed my heart posture before Him. Honestly, I was not ready. There was a lot that needed to be taught to me and I was not in position or prepared. I was just a HOT TOT. Seriously, I was!

Reason #4: I thought I would finally attract the right guy. Boy, was I wrong! The ones I met online were worse than the men I met at the local grocery store, restaurants, malls, etc. I ended up being so unequally yoked with the men I conversed with it was not even funny. I remember meeting this guy for dinner. We met in a public place because he was NOT picking me up from my home. I've had too many men showing up to my home unannounced (that's a story for another day). After dinner, we sat in his car for a little after dinner conversation. Baby, that was a bad idea. This young man smelled like sex and weed. While in the restaurant I sat across from him and could not smell him. Being in that non-ventilated area caused your girl's nose to become offended! I cut the conversation short and made up some excuse to get out the car. Homeboy had the nerve to get out the car in order to give me a hug. I was not happy about that. He then grabbed me and leaned in for a kiss. I quickly moved away from him. I told him to have a good night while I jumped in my car.

Reason #5: Mental health. There really are some ill people out here in the world. I honestly believe everyone should have some type of psychological exam completed before setting up an online dating profile. Texting or talking to someone on the phone doesn't really show you a person's mental health status. It is their actions and words. I've learned that when you first start talking to a person, they put on their best self. After times goes on and allowing the Holy Spirit to speak to you about the individual, you will begin to see what's in their heart. Out of the abundance of the heart the mouth speaks (Matthew 12:34). I've always heard the saying, "Everything that glitters ain't gold." Isn't that the truth. It was the men I found extremely attractive that were mentally unstable. I would use the word crazy, but I do not want to offend anyone. Another thing I learned was that even though the glitter did not shine that much, I still looked.

Reason #6: I was not Holy Spirit-led, I was Keisha-led. I was straight carnal. I wanted to satisfy my flesh. I thought since I was done with graduate school it was my time to mingle... and that I did! I mingled myself into some dead-end dating

31

relationships; relationships that I should have cut off 3 months into the "getting-to-know- you" phase- especially after the Holy Spirit was saying to me, "He's not your husband."

These are just a few reasons why I kissed online dating goodbye (although there are many more). If you find it's still an option for you, make sure you're sensitive to the Spirit and any red flags!

Shalom & Agape,

Keisha

Day 14

As I Continue to Wait

May 20, 2017

On December 28, 2016, I received a prophesy from my pastor at the time during a revival. He opened his mouth, then said, "WAIT," and spelled out W-A-I-T. That was NOT the word I wanted to hear from the Lord. Who wants to be told to wait? Not me!

As humans we tend to want things quick, fast, and in a hurry. That's why a lot of us use the microwave instead of the oven to cook our food. Why? Because we do not like waiting patiently for things to cook thoroughly. For me in this season, patience has been my virtue.

In the past, waiting was not a strong area for me. I've always had an impatient personality. Going through the process of being prepared, positioned, and now waiting on God to lead me regarding marriage was a struggle. I was the type of person where if I wanted something right then and there, I was going to get it and have it. You could say that I was an impulsive person when it came down to certain things; however, as I've continued to walk with Yeshua (Jesus), patience has had its perfect work within me (James 1:4). It has definitely been a journey. Scripture says, "But let patience have its perfect work, that you may be perfect and complete, lacking nothing." James 1:4 NKJV. I can attest to that: I lack nothing!

The closer I get to the beginning of my new endeavor the more content I feel within my heart. I am sober in my mind and my emotions. While I WAIT, I am expecting God to richly supply much for me in every area of my life for the rest of my life. I was not a fan of the journey in the beginning; however, if it wasn't for this journey, I would not be in the place I am with Yeshua (Jesus). I love Abba Father God, Yeshua (Jesus), and the Holy Spirit who are 3 in 1.

In the end, I know it will be worth the WAIT.

Shalom & Agape,

Keisha

Wife in Training while Waiting. Pray for me as I pray for you!

Day 15

I Need Jesus

June 30, 2017

At the end of the day, I need Jesus. It does not matter how long I have been walking, pursuing, or building my relationship with Jesus; I need Him daily. Each day I have to consciously welcome Jesus and the Holy Spirit. The process of being a wife in training is an ongoing one.

I also need Him in other areas of my life; I need Him to assist me with my finances, my relationships, deliver and help me manage my soul issues, and of course for my spirit-man. In Jesus is where I find the balance that I need. To someone looking outside-in they would say that I'm overly zealous and "unbalanced." The truth is that I am completely balanced with Jesus because the things of this world do not weigh me down. I was conversing with the Holy Spirit and He gave me truth on what it means to be balanced in Him. 1 Peter 5:7 explains it all, "Casting all your care upon him; for he careth for you." If I am casting fear, worry, stress, anxiety or anything that causes me to feel weighted, I've given it all to Yeshua Himself, Jesus the Christ. So, if I'm doing that balance is coming to me through Him.

Give me Jesus! I need Him!

Shalom & Agape,

Keisha

Day 16

30 Years and Counting

July 31, 2017

On 7/15/2017, my parents celebrated their 30th year wedding anniversary. To watch two people, grow daily from marriage has been such a blessing to me. I've seen them at their lowest and now at the place of true happiness and contentment. Once I fully understood the institution of marriage and watching my parents grow, I've learned that my parents were two servants coming together to serve each other for the rest of their lives. Watching my parents over the past 30 years has shown me that marriage is about sacrificial love and learning how to meet each other in the middle. It's also about being a team. Honestly, there is not an "I" in team. They taught me what WE, US, and OUR looks like.

Scripture say that love is... Love is patient. Love is kind. Is not jealous. Love does not brag. Is not arrogant. Does not act unbecomingly. It does not seek its own. Is not provoked.

Does not take into account the wrong suffered. Does not rejoice in unrighteousness. Rejoices with the truth. Bears all things. Believes all things. Hopes all things. Endures all things. Love never fails. (1 Corinthians 13:4-8 NASB).

My parents have not crossed every T nor dotted every I; however, I've seen them grow in the scriptures above.

From my parents' union, I've learned much about them as well as myself. My prayer for them is that they see another 30 years according to God's will... in Jesus name. Amen.

Shalom & Agape,

Keisha

Day 17

Sorry, Not Sorry.

September 19, 2017

I will CUT you off and keep it pushing. You don't know me. Recently, I was challenged with the comment that basically referred to me as being too spiritual, and that I would conform if pursued by a certain individual. Let me be honest: 4 years ago, I compromised— not conformed. I remember talking to this guy. I was really digging him although deep within myself I knew he was NOT the one for me. I remember hearing the voice of the Holy Spirit. He said, "He is NOT your husband." Me, being who I am said, "You're right, he's not yet." By this time, we had been talking for about 3-4 months. Because I did not want to be by myself anymore and I enjoyed the attention that I was getting from him, I kept him around. Unfortunately, things kept coming up between us. People would ask what we were doing, and I would just stand there with a blank face like, "Ask him." The Lord had mercy on me because I kept that man around for way too long.

Looking back, I compromised more than I conformed to what he thought I should be and do. He (the guy) also said that he did not want to intrude on what God was doing for me; therefore, choosing not to commit. Personally, I believe that was a copout because he did not want to give up certain coping mechanisms that he learned to due to childhood trauma that led into his adult years. I understand how it's easy to remain complacent and comfortable. I've never been the one to become comfortable with being complacent though.

One thing the Holy Spirit taught me years ago is that conforming is seen as being normal or average and I'm not normal - I'm supernatural. Anything pertaining to my life is not normal or the average because I walk with Jesus Christ. If anything, I would remove you out my life before I conform to whom people think I should.

"And do not be conformed to this world, but be transformed by the renewing of your mind..." Romans 12:2 NASB). Daily my mind is renewed, so I will NEVER conform. I'm made in the image of God, so I live from the Kingdom of God. I live from the supernatural. The supernatural is the norm for my life. A lot of people may not agree with that, but I do not care. I know who God; Jesus and the Holy Spirit have been in my life. Some may call it strange, but I call it living by faith.

Shalom & Agape,

Keisha

Day 18

Happy 1 Year #WifeinTraining

October 4, 2017

Dear Reader,

As I was celebrating #WifeinTraining's one-year blog anniversary over the weekend, I came across a fake #wifeintraining Twitter account called wifetraininginmn. I was devastated to learn that someone would mock a move of God relating to building the body of Christ, sharing my process and journey. On top of all of that, the person also opened another twitter account pretending to be me. Talk about feeling emotional! Never in a million years would I think that someone would do something so mean to me. I know that I can't be friends with everyone, but why would someone try this? Those were my thoughts. I don't mess with anyone. I stay in my own lane and I don't go looking for trouble. I've never been that type of person. After much thought and praying about the fake twitter accounts, two things arose:

Forgiveness and healing. It hurts my heart to see that someone would come against and mock a move of God. My heart goes out to the individual mocking me, my values, beliefs, and my God. If I could give the individual a hug just to let them know they are loved, I would.

My prayer is this: I pray in the name of Jesus Christ that every individual reading this post will experience the love of God in a greater measure. I pray that you will receive healing from being rejected, from bitterness, and forgive those who have wronged you in any way. In Jesus Christ's name, amen.

Shalom & Agape,

Keisha

Day 19

Letter to My Husband

October 18, 2017

My beloved (future) husband,

Words cannot express the joy and peace that comes to me knowing that you are being prepared for our (future) family. I can sense your closeness even though you are somewhere walking the earth. God has truly blessed our family with such an amazing man as yourself. You definitely know how to comfort me when I need to be comforted. You've learned how to cover and carry me in prayer even when I get on your nerves. Love you, babe! Your skin has been kissed by the sun. Your lips are soft as silk on a warm summer night in Spain. Your voice is the sound of the ocean calming to my soul. Hearing you speak stirs my spirit and my soul. Resting on your bosom, hearing your heart whisper in my ear brings great peace to me. You are the king of our home. Once you speak shalom, the atmosphere listens and there's peace. I pray that you will continue to cover me in prayer as I continue to cover you in prayer.

Love Your Wife & Queen - Shalom & Agape,

Keisha

Day 20

Tunnel Vision

November 15, 2017

As I continue to actively pursue walking in the fullness of God through Jesus Christ with the help of the Holy Spirit, I'm realizing that I have to have tunnel vision. It has been one heck of a journey to get to this place. Fortunately, I know that I am more focused than I've even been. I would allow my relationships with people- specifically romantic relationships - hold me back from walking in everything that God desires me to walk in. Even though I desire marriage and everything it entails, that's not at the forefront of my mind or what I see. I know that in God's timing all that will come. I'm focused and God will NOT put me to shame.

"Let your eyes look directly ahead and let you gaze be fixed straight in front of you." Proverbs 4:25 NASB

"Fear not, for you will not be put to shame; and do not feel humiliated, for you will not be disgraced." (Isaiah 54:4a NASB)

Shalom & Agape,

Keisha

Day 21

Reflection Revealed Many Victories

January 12, 2018

Whew! Finally, 2 0 1 8 is here! As I reflect on 2017, I will admit it was a very intense year for me; from being challenged spiritually to staying loving in relationships with people who've done me straight bogus. Twenty-seventeen has definitely humbled me in every area of my life. Even with all the humbling, the Holy Spirit taught me very valuable lessons. He taught me that my relationship with Him is very key and important for me to be effective in relationships in both my personal and professional life. He also taught me that prayer and fasting is important. If it wasn't for the fasting (humbling oneself before <u>Abba</u>) and the praying, I honestly do NOT know where I would be or what I would be doing. I probably would be backslidden somewhere because of all the pressure. Thankfully, He surrounded me with strong individuals who were able to push me through some of the darkest moments in my life. Even with everything that was taking place in my life in 2017, I was able to remain focused to the point that God, Himself, helped me to create and birth some pretty awesome things. He gave me the vision for t-shirts to go along with this blog, which were released in July; He then gave a vision to have a bachelorette party. We (my team #theMRS) trail blazed through that with the planning and execution with the Holy Spirit leading us. He was definitely the One helping me to overcome the adversity and opposition. It is funny how we believe that just because we are in Christ, we will not have to deal with much. The truth is we do deal with A LOT because we are in Christ. "In the world you have tribulation, but take courage." John 16:33. The beautiful thing about it all is that Christ's spirit is with me, you, and everyone else who believe.

He also gave me the hashtag #theMRStribe. At first, I had no idea what the MRS stood for except a married woman. I even printed business cards with the hashtag! He gave the words to my cousin who then gave the words to me: Manifested Relational Success. Sounds fancy, huh? Mind you, all of this was happening while I was going through the fire of maturity. Talk about uncomfortable. It was the grace of God that got me through. Whew!

Twenty-seventeen was definitely a year I do not want to repeat. Guess what, I won't!

I was V I C T O R I O U S in 2017 and 2 0 1 8 is a MEGA year and a year of DOMINATION.

I'm ready for what is coming. Will you continue to join me as I embark on this journey?

Shalom & Agape,

Keisha

Day 22

Hello LOVE

January 19, 2018

Hello love, as I continue to embark on this journey of preparing to be a kingdom wife, I've came across many challenges. Since the beginning of this journey, I've always desired some type of normalcy in my life relating to "dating." With the way my relationship with God is currently set-up and His jealousy for me, I don't think I'll have the normalcy I desire. I've finally accepted that on 1/14/18. I have also yielded myself completely to Abba including the normalcy I desire in dating. Honestly, I thought I would have been married two years ago to this guy I met in 2015. From my perspective, I thought things were lining up for us to be married. I was open to what I believed God wanted for us. The truth was that we both were overwhelmed with sexual chemistry and we lacked effective communication skills that was needed at the time. Another thing that we did not discuss was the desired outcome between us. Yes, we both desired marriage but we did not really take the time to learn each other's communication style. I also had unrealistic expectations. In my mind I had pictured how he would pursue me, how our courtship would look, and how life would be with him all planned out. Let's talk about how unrealistic that was! The sad part was that I desired marriage more than I desired God. I didn't even know that until Holy Spirit revealed that to me. Talk about heartbroken. I was hurt and sick because I LOVE God so much.

You're probably wondering what does my title, 'Hello, love' have to do with anything I'm writing about. Truth be told it has a lot to do with love. We as humans love to feel love. Humans say things like, "I like to feel that you love me," or, "the love vibe between us is right." Let me help us all out: love is not based off your feelings, my feelings, or anyone else's feelings. Love is truly based off 1 Corinthians 13:4-7. Love is action! I'm still working on my love towards people and working on not provoking or challenging (Galatians 5:26) someone who I say I love. The Lord Jesus Christ through the Holy Spirit is truly helping me by helping manage my emotions while I continue adulthood. There have been many times where I have provoked and challenged intentionally. Thinking back on it, I should not have done that. Oh well. I had to learn somehow in order to help others. For Kingdom and for glory!

Daily, I'm seeing this love walk in a new way. I was recently cut deep with love being patient, meaning long-suffering. To be honest, who likes to suffer long in any situation? Not me. Growing up I would learn from other people's situations or learning/growing experiences. Anything that would hurt me or look like it would hurt me, I would go the other way saying, "I'm good."

Another part of the verse that says love does not take into account a wrong suffered. I was cut deep on that, too. It made me confront and challenge the saying that most black people say, "I forgive you, but I'm not going to forget." Listen here, you better forget that situation because if you don't, you are keeping record of a wrong suffered against you and that goes against a Kingdom principle. Not only that- when you do forgive and forget you don't allow yourself to be tormented or entertained by bitterness, unforgiveness, and jealousy.

Going back to this man, he and I struggled because from my perspective we didn't know how to communicate to get an understanding from one another. Also, my personality and spirit are strong so I just knew (prideful eye) I had it altogether and there was nothing wrong with me. Hahahahaha. I WAS COMPLETELY WRONG. Wow, I admitted that. Whoa! Much growth has taken place with me. I'm just being honest and transparent. I'm taking the mask all the way off. I'm far from perfect. If you would have asked me that three years ago, I would have said, "What do you mean? I'm perfect and I would marry me." NOT. Looking back, I needed a complete heart makeover... you know, the works. I'm saying hello to love again with a mind that is being transformed and renewed daily (Romans 12:2).

Love you all - Shalom & Agape,

Keisha

Day 23

Love is more than a feeling...

January 27, 2018

"I believe when a person shows us their love through action, it causes our bodies to respond to the act of love as an emotion. I believe that is a reason why people associate love as a feeling."

Shalom & Agape,

Keisha

Answer these questions:

What does it mean to you to love?

What does it mean to you to be loved?

Day 24

#theUnmasking

February 19, 2018

The UNmasking of me has been so uneasy. Sitting in the presence of God has caused many tears to flow like rivers down my face. Getting naked before God makes me feel very vulnerable. I have no other choice but to be that way with Him. As God continues to make me into the wife He desires for me to be for my husband, being vulnerable and transparent has been something I've been pushed into. Being naked before God has caused me to feel cold even though He's an all-consuming fire. I was so used to wearing layers that I forgot what it felt like to be UNmasked and naked before the Lord. Now I'm sitting here in His presence desiring more of Him even with all my nakedness. I guess there's nothing to be ashamed about when being UNmasked and naked before His throne.

Let me paint a picture for you: the unmasking of me is God exposing the condition of my heart as well as my motives. My motives haven't always been pure. I wanted to be married so that I could have sex "legally." So, being unmasked in that area was embarrassing. However, because God unmasked certain areas of my heart, He was able to right what was wrong within my heart, my soul, and spirit.

"But we all, with unveiled face, beholding as in a mirror the glory of the Lord, are being transformed into the same image from glory to glory, just as from the Lord, the Spirit." (2 Corinthians 3:18 NASB).

Yours in Christ - Shalom & Agape,

Keisha

Day 25

Saying I Love You

February 26, 2018

One day, it was placed on my heart to send a friend the words "I love you" twice a day (morning and night). At first, I was hesitant because I did not know how the person was going to respond. To be honest, I was reluctant to sending the message. I did not know if they were even going to say it back. All I knew was that I was given an order and I wanted to obey. The first two days were difficult because of my own pride and ego. As the days continued to pass by; me saying "I love you" began to soften my heart. Whew. I wasn't expecting that at all. I felt the love of Abba God at a deeper level. How, you may ask? Well, that deep level of love felt like the warm hug you receive from a grandparent you haven't seen in a while. It's a love that I've never experienced before from anyone- not even my own parents-and I know they love me. This type of love I experienced shifted my whole perspective of what it means to love, be loved, and be in love. Hearing Abba say, "I

LOVE YOU," through one of His prophets had me in tears. Even as I write this, I can feel the love of my Heavenly Father. *sigh* To be at this place was something I longed for and I thought it would have been a person I can physically see and touch who will display that to me. Nope, not so. Abba God had other plans.

What I learned from this is that when God tells you to do something, it for you. What God did for me was soften my heart, healed me, and delivered me from myself (pride and ego). However, softening my heart, healing my soul, and delivering me from my pride and ego is a continuum.

My prayer is that you will experience the love of Abba God at a deeper level by Holy Spirit through Jesus Christ. Amen.

Shalom & Agape,

Keisha

Answer these questions:

Have you ever felt an incline to say "I love you" to someone who made you angry and hurt you?

If so, how did you feel saying it to them?

What was their response?

Day 26

A Prideful Heart

May 12, 2018

Listen here, when the Lord began to minister to my heart about pride and the lack of being submissive, it took me clean out. Now I see where pride was hiding in my heart. When it came down to submitting to certain people, I wouldn't. I would be quick to give the side-eye. Since then I've learned the true meaning of what it means to submit, honor, and respect. As a wife, submitting to my husband as he's submitted to God is key. Also, honor and respect is something I desire to bring to him daily. I've learned that honor and respect is what a man- specifically my husband- desires. My prayer is this: Abba will continue to search my heart and reveal me to me. I turn away from this prideful heart of mine. Create in me a clean heart oh God, and renew a right spirit within me (Psalm 51:10). I also pray that I will continue to bring honor and respect to my husband in the name of Jesus Christ. Amen.

Shalom & Agape,

Keisha

Day 27

Marriage

May 20, 2018

As I continue to age, I have learned that many individuals have at some time struggled with consistency, commitment, transparency, communication, etc. As I continue working on keeping my "yes" to Christ, I've noticed that there are times when I have in the past struggled with being consistent with my communication with Him and remaining transparent. Striving to keep my "yes" has become challenging especially relating to marriage for me. In the past, marriage was once an idol to me and I didn't know it until the Holy Spirit revealed it to me. Also, in the past I would have taken things into my own hands and started dating the wrong men. You're probably thinking there is nothing wrong with dating. Actually, you are absolutely correct that there is nothing wrong with dating. Dating just for the fun of it can become dangerous. I have done that. I've engaged myself with men that I knew I had no future with. Because I was bored and needed to fill voids at that time, I would step out, ending back where I started... at the feet of Jesus.

Although I may have posted this before in a previous blog, it bears repeating: I have to commit to Jesus Christ first before I can commit to, remain consistent with, be transparent to, and effectively communicate with anyone— especially a future spouse. Does the thought of marriage terrify me? Absolutely. Does the thought of marrying a person who isn't a destiny partner scare me? Heck yea. However, the word of God says perfect loves casts out fear. As God continues to perfect His love in me and for my future spouse there is nothing to worry about, right? Wrong. It's wrong because no one is perfect and that's why we came to Christ in the first place. I can only speak for myself, that it was His agape (unconditional) love that caught my attention. Through Christ, God has continued to show me His love for me. Sigh. As I continue to say "yes" to Jesus the more I'm continuing to become one with Him and dying daily to become one with the Bridegroom who is my husband. Now, that's marriage: dying to yourself daily to become one with the other.

Daily dying to become one with Christ...

Shalom & Agape,

Keisha

Day 28

It's Been A While... Hey Y'all!

August 12, 2018

For the last few months I have been busy with many transitions. One of those transitions was moving to another state. You've read that correctly: I have relocated to Houston, TX! Let me tell you, this has been a crazy journey. I am still in awe and disbelief. I NEVER would have thought to quit my job, move away from my family and close friends, and move to another state. I knew that I wanted to change positions but moving really wasn't at the top of my list. Moving to Texas was only a thought, now that thought turned into my reality. I'm HERE now!

Let me give you a little back story about how Texas was even on the map for me. About twelve years ago a friend of mine and I were talking, and they mentioned that they saw Texas for me. I said to them, "Texas?" They said, "Yes, and I see the continent Africa." Of course, I was puzzled by the Africa comment. I didn't dismiss it. At that time, I'd never been to Texas. I always felt some type of connection not knowing that Texas would be my home in the future.

Six years went by and I ended up traveling to South Africa and Namibia. How did I end up there!? I ended up studying abroad for about two weeks and it changed my life. Six years after my trip to Africa, I moved to Texas. This move was not one of those moves where my mind was completely made up about it. Thoughts of moving thousands of miles away from my family would leave me speechless and crying off/on at least twice a week. Everything I was familiar with was in Minnesota. Actually, a year ago around this time, I drove a friend down to Dallas, TX for her big move. Even then someone said to me I was going to be the next one to move to Texas. Of course, I was in straight denial. I did NOT want to hear that I would be moving away from my family, friends, jobs, etc. I was in denial for about another four to five months. So, I started preparing myself for my move- or I thought I was preparing myself. I informed my landlord at the time that I was not interested in signing a new lease. My lease was up in mid-March and I was not going to sign another one. Talk about faith moves! My landlord put me on a month-to-month lease with a 60-day notice move out date. Even then I was not sure when I was moving.

The month of May rolls up on me. I ended up getting a roommate towards the end of April. People who know me know that I was NOT looking for a roommate. Let's talk about being a WIFE IN TRAINING! This journey has definitely been a humbling one. Nothing against my roommate but I haven't had one since undergrad at the University of Minnesota.

I knew that there were some things in me that needed to be worked out, confronted, and dealt with in order for me to move on to the next which was Texas. It was hard seeing the heart issues that I have because of life's past hurts and disappointments, and from even the most influential people in my life from my parents to leaders. No one was excluded from this. I'm learning, growing, and loving, which is super uncomfortable, by the way. I've embraced it and grow from that uncomfortable place. To be honest, I'm still in that uncomfortable place. The way God does things, I'm probably going to be there for a while. *sigh*

Growing in more way than one and healing from the inside out.

Shalom & Agape,

Keisha

Day 29

This Can't Be Real

September 28, 2018

The Most Difficult 72 Hours EVER!
This past weekend has been one for the books for my family and me. On Friday, September 20, I found out that my great-uncle passed away, one of my aunts home was broken into while she was at work (thank goodness she wasn't home); my grandmother was admitted to the hospital for a mild heart attack; and then Sunday 9/23, I found out one of my male cousins shot himself in the head. Let's talk about the TRAUMA.

With the series of events that had happened this past weekend, I didn't know if I should lay in the fetal position in my bed or grab my bible to meditate on Matthew 5:4 that reads, "Blessed are those who mourn, for they shall be comforted." As you can tell, I decided to grab my bible. I also made a picture to post it on my Instagram (IG) page. I seriously can feel the prayers from very one who have laid or said a prayer on my family and I's behalf. I thank God for every last one of you.

As we prepare to lay my great-uncle to rest this week, questions of him flood my thoughts: Was his soul satisfied with how his life went? Did he forgive those that he needed to forgive? Did he make it into heaven? To be honest, I don't have or know the answers to those questions. All I can really do is trust God.

After finding out my great-uncles passing, I then found out that my aunt's home was broken into. I truly thank God that no one was home. Even though it wasn't my home, I still felt violated and offended that someone would stoop so low to break into my aunt's home. Fortunately, the person did not take anything from my aunt's home, just broke a window or two. From my understanding, the person cut them self really badly and their blood was all over the place. I honestly pray that they didn't hurt themselves too bad. Yea, I know it sounds weird that I'm praying for this individual, but God loves everyone- even the ones who man cannot deal with. My heart goes out to the person. My prayer for them is that they heal from the physical and emotional scars that life has put on them in the name of Jesus Christ. Amen.

Now, on to my grandma (whom I used to call my girl). I don't know where to begin, to be honest. All I know is that I wish I was in Minnesota on Friday to just sit with her. The thought of my grandma having a heart attack makes me so sad. I know heart attacks are seen as physical; however, I would like to challenge your thinking. I believe your emotional state affects your physical well-being. Do I know exactly what my grandma is dealing with emotionally? No. I know that depression and anxiety run on my mother's side of the family and that's why I choose the way of Jesus Christ by casting all my cares on Him. I'm literally throwing all of my concerns of this world to Him. I definitely cannot carry this stuff. In regard to my grandma being admitted to the hospital, I quickly gave all my concerns regarding that to Christ. I'd rather not carry that. I prayed and know He's taking care of it, especially these emotions of mine.

Let's talk about Sunday, the day my cousin passed. It was reported that he killed himself. Finding out about the death of my cousin hit my heart hard as he was young and left behind a beautiful daughter. I later found out he suffered from depression—although no one knew that he was suicidal until the day it happened. Then I also thought about my brothers. I also began to think about all of the black men who suffer from some type of mental health disorder and don't even know it and they self- medicate by abusing mood-altering substances. My prayer is that more men will address their mental health more. It saddens me to see them suffer in silence.

This is why praying for my (future) husband's mental health along with protection has been such an important part of my journey of becoming a wife. Something the Holy Spirit taught me that has stuck out to me was to cover my husband in prayer due to having to deal with the world. I also know that after a long day of dealing with the world I have to ensure that he's protected and our home is a peaceful environment.

I pray that God will give my family and I strength and peace during this difficult time, in Jesus name. Amen.

Shalom & Agape,

Keisha

Day 30

Remain Silent, He will Fight for You

October 3, 2018

It's okay to not accept certain words and behavior.

This past week I have been tested by many things. My prayer is that I "pass the test," because some people just don't have boundaries, or they do weird and spooky stuff. Dear sir/ma'am before calling or sending me a text message please get direction from the Holy Spirit because your timing has been off.

I'm learning that I do not have to accept anything from anyone. I do not have to accept people's behavior. I do not have to accept their words. I recently received a message from someone whom I haven't spoken to in months. After reading the message several times, I made a decision not to respond to the person. I even went to block and delete them from Facebook. You may be asking why did she choose to not respond, then block and delete the person? Answer: I just buried my great-uncle and I did not feel like dealing with any mess concerning whatever it was. Grieving the loss of two family members and the fact that my grandmother had a heart attack had been heavy on me. Therefore, I decided not to accept what the person had to say. The sad part is that I had (past tense), a friendship with them (or so I thought) for over 20 years.

I was extremely disappointed and hurt by the way the person approached me. The person didn't say, "Hey Keisha, I read that you're grieving the loss of family... I'm sending you my condolences." Nope, that is not the salutation I received. I received a text message regarding a dream that they had. Sir/Ma'am, I do not want hear about the dream you had and got it "interpreted." Did you actually ask the Holy Spirit or did you go straight to man to give you an understanding? Not only that, Holy Spirit did not allow you to discern if the time was even appropriate to say anything to me. Sir/Ma'am please get off my phone line and do not text me. I do not want to hear anything you have to say about a dream. I'm grieving the loss of a couple of family members. Bye Lance! (that's not the person's name, but I hope you get it).

Choosing to not respond, blocking, and then deleting them was something I would not have done a year ago. A year ago, I would have just accepted the behavior, their words, and allowed the words from them just replay in my mind and continue to re-read the text message they sent me. Nope, not this time. I deleted the whole text thread and blocked their number from my phone. Even still, I chose to forgive them because I do not need anything in my heart towards them or anyone else, they are connected to. I know that God will defend me, according to Exodus 14:14, "The LORD will fight for you while you keep silent." NASB.

Trust and believe it's hard for me to remain silent. However, as a wife in training, I know there will be times when the Holy Spirit will prompt me to remain quiet and allow Him to speak to my husband's heart. For this situation saying less or remaining silent is speaking more volumes than me responding. Enough is enough. I'm learning not to accept people's words and behavior towards me. Establishing boundaries and sustaining boundaries may seem harsh to those who have never experienced me having them; however, it is something that has protected me from becoming offended from other's behavior.

One thing is for sure, I definitely do not have the emotional energy to entertain anyone who wants to come at me with some six to nine-month-old mess. Please just leave me alone. Healing from the inside out and loving God.

Shalom & Agape,

Keisha

Prayer:
My prayer is that you will allow God to fight for you as you remain silent in the name of Jesus Christ. Amen.

Day 31

It's Been Over A Week

October 10, 2018 (my grandma's B-Day)

I've been in Minnesota for over a week now. Honestly, all I can think about it going back home to Houston, Texas. Even though I've only been gone from Minnesota for two months, I miss Houston like I've lived there my whole life. I guess I'm definitely connected to my new home.

I have a few more days before I return home to Houston and I'm excited about getting back there. Yes, I am going to miss my family in Minnesota but, Texas is home to me now. I definitely thought it would have taken more time for me to adapt to the culture, weather, traffic (not just during rush hour, lol), etc. Fortunately, I'm doing very well. All thanks belong to God!

My reasons for going back to Minnesota was due to the two deaths in my family and my grandma having a mild heart attack. Despite those events, the day before leaving to get back to Houston, I attended a baby shower and celebrated my aunts and grandma's birthdays. Reflecting on dinner I had with my family makes my heart smile. We were able to just enjoy one another freely. We laughed, laughed and laughed some more. We were a little loud, but that comes along with having 18 people sitting at a table to have dinner. It brought me much joy to be able to spend time with them.

For the record, I really do **MISS** my family. However, Houston is now home. Home is where the heart is, right? Well, for me it is. As I continue to reflect on the journey of becoming a wife or being in training, I'm learning that this process has been a journey of my heart; seeing the ugly parts of me. It has been difficult. Some days are easier than the others. However, I've made it to this point: in this place of contentment, wholeness and where my home (heart) is in a healthy place. I will continue this journey by embracing it while allowing the Holy Spirit to show me my heart condition. I pray that my heart will remain in that healthy place.

Healing daily, loving God, and sustaining boundaries...

Shalom & Agape,

Keisha

About the Author

LaKeisha L. Wells who goes by Keisha L. Wells is a woman who seeks to inspire young adult women through her blog, W.I.T Movement, and her life's experiences. Keisha received her Bachelor's in Family Social Science from the University of Minnesota-Twin Cities and her Master of Social Work focusing on Program Development, Policy, and Administration from Augsburg University formally Augsburg College. She pursued her career as a social worker helping many individuals regain a sense of purpose. While she understands that she can't reach everyone, she sets her focus on the one she can help. Keisha has used her compassion to serve those in her community as a social worker. She continues to seek out opportunities to serve people with love as her driving force. She desires to see women from all walks of life reach their fullest potential in God. I Pray in Jesus' Name was birthed from the belief that everyone is accepted and loved by God and that He hears them. She believes there is nothing that can stand in the way of her becoming all that God destined for her to be and she also believes the same for you!